Succe
Training
in a week

Malcolm Peel

Headway · Hodder & Stoughton

658.3124

$\stackrel{\circ}{i}\mathbf{\mathit{\mathit{ll}}}$ *the Institute*
 of Management

F O U N D A T I O N

The Institute of Management (IM) is at the forefront of management development and best management practice. The Institute embraces all levels of management from students to chief executives. It provides a unique portfolio of services for all managers, enabling them to develop skills and achieve management excellence.

For information on the benefits of membership, please contact:

Department HS
Institute of Management
Cottingham Road
Corby
Northants NN17 1TT

Tel. 0536 204222 Fax 0536 201651

This series is commissioned by the Institute of Management Foundation.

British Library Cataloguing in Publication Data

ISBN 0 340 61889 2

First published 1994
Impression number 10 9 8 7 6 5 4 3 2 1
Year   1999 1998 1997 1996 1995 1994

Typeset by Multiplex Techniques Ltd, St Mary Cray, Kent.
Printed for Hodder & Stoughton Educational, a division of Hodder Headline Plc, 338 Euston Road, London NW1 3BH by Colorcraft Ltd, Hong Kong

CONTENTS

Training is universally agreed to be a key to success; success for individuals, for organisations, and for the whole economy. Everyone trains others in their everyday life. As parents, we train our children. As people with experience and knowledge in our domestic, leisure and working lives, we pass these on to others who can benefit from them. As supervisors and managers we train those who work for us.

This book is designed to give the reader a general appreciation of all aspects of training, and also to improve his or her training skills. Its approach is based on vocational training; i.e. training within the working situation. However, much of what is said can be applied to training in sport, leisure activities, and other areas.

We shall take a step in the process each day of the week. The steps are:

Sunday	An overview: the training sequence
Monday	Assessing the need for training
Tuesday	Choice of method I: requirements for effective training
Wednesday	Choice of method II: types of training method
Thursday	Designing a training course
Friday	Course delivery
Saturday	Use of training, evaluation, and sources of help

Training and development – an overview

Today, we will set training in perspective, consider what it is, why it is important and who and what is involved. We shall look at:

- What is training?
- Why training is important
- Commitment to training
- The training sequence

What is training?

To many people, the word 'training' conjures up a group sitting in a classroom listening to a lecture; 'training' can all too easily be thought of as attendance on a course. But courses are only one kind of training, and will not always be the most effective. 'Training' is a much broader activity:

A definition of training
Any activity designed to improve another individual's performance in a specific area.

We will therefore think of training as an activity that has an agent – the trainer – and one or more recipients – the trainees.

Development

'Development' is a closely related word. Indeed, 'development and training' are frequently used in double harness. We develop throughout life, rapidly or slowly, well or badly as a result of all our experiences. Training is one of the ways development occurs, but there are many others. These other influences may be more powerful; good training, for example, may be cancelled out by negative experiences. We may be trained to do a job well, then work with a boss or others who do it badly, and pick up their bad ways. To be effective, training must be supported by the other influences that affect our development: our own priorities, the way we are managed, the behaviour of our colleagues and the rewards we are given, the culture of our organisation and of society.

Education

The difference between training and education is blurred, and the two often overlap. Education is generally knowledge based; training aims to change behaviour, usually by developing skills. Education is broader and longer term in its objectives; to learn about English literature, for example, will affect us all our lives. Training may be narrower; to learn the use of a specific computer software package, perhaps, or how to operate a particular machine. Education is not specifically aimed at earning a living, although it may help to do this; geography, history or music are more likely to enrich our life rather than provide hard cash. Training is more likely to be related to our vocation; we may train as a secretary, an accountant or an HGV driver.

There has been a long-running debate as to how far education should be vocational. British schools have long guided the brightest pupils into academic, non-vocational studies. Many of the older, established universities regarded vocational studies as inferior. Since the establishment of the polytechnics in the 1960s and their upgrading to university status in the 1990s, this balance has tilted.

Learning
Trainers often use the word 'learning' in phrases such as a 'learning experience', a 'learning situation' – even a 'learning company'. The implication is that training and education will only succeed if the trainee wants to learn. In a free society, the trainer or educator can only provide the opportunity and environment for learning; it is up to the individual to take it from there.

Why training is important

The benefits of training cannot be taken for granted. Some people regard it as a waste of time, and a distraction from more important activities. Many have undergone little or no training during their working life, and do not feel the lack of it. Some employers and managers see training as an expense they can ill afford, and as the first to be cut when money gets tight.

But good training has always been important, and now matters more than ever. No one can now learn all they will need for their career at its start. Whatever kind of work we do, it will change. Changes come from many causes:

Why jobs need new skills
- Technological development
- Changed systems or procedures
- Changes in customers' needs
- New regulations or legislation
- Environmental changes
- New materials
- New products or services

Technological development alone produces a continuing need for training.

The effects of technological development
Most jobs used to be unskilled, or needed only simple skills; manual work in factories, in building and on the farm; clerical tasks in the office. It was possible for most people to earn a reasonable living without acquiring complex skills.

This is no longer true. Every year, machinery takes over more unskilled work. Manual work is done by machine; the navvy of last century has been replaced by the JCB of today. The mechanically emptied wheely-bin has replaced the manually emptied dustbin. The washing-up is done by an electric dishwasher. Much office work is done by machine; electronic information technology has replaced the ledger, the quill pen and office stool. Records are kept, sorted and found on electronic databases. Accounts are prepared by computers. Letters are produced by word processing and sent by fax.

Whilst technology is reducing the number of unskilled jobs available it is increasing the number of jobs that require high level skills. The numerically controlled machine tool, the multi-voltage electric locomotive, and the computer network are complex and need highly skilled people to design, build, operate and service them.

Technology is also now changing at an ever-increasing rate. Until recent years, it was possible to acquire the skills needed for a lifetime of work near its beginning; to become, for example, a skilled blacksmith by serving an apprenticeship. Skills could also be developed over a long period of time. A railway engine driver, for example, would learn his job over many years. He would begin cleaning engines, graduate to firing them, and finally to driving progressively more important trains. He would reach the 'top link' jobs, driving principle expresses, only after half a life-time of work.

Today, in almost all jobs, this is no longer true. No sooner have we acquired one set of skills, than technology moves on and new equipment or techniques become available. If we do not learn the new skills these require, we will soon become out of date. Training is no longer something we do once for a life-time; it is something we must do continuously throughout our life.

The increasing pace of change affects those who drop out of a career (to raise a family, for example, or to travel abroad) with special force. There are now few jobs which it is possible to leave for, say, 10 years and pick up again without retraining.

The value of training
Training is of value to the individual trainee, the employer, and society as a whole.

Training is vital to us as individuals. Most jobs for the untrained are badly paid, low level, and boring. They offer little chance of promotion; they lead nowhere. Such jobs are getting fewer, and the gap between them and jobs for trained people is getting bigger.

Badly trained breadwinners can support only a poor life-style for their family. Untrained parents are less able and less likely to ensure their children are well trained. This is a vicious circle that can limit the achievement of one generation after another; the 'cycle of deprivation'.

Employers need a well-trained workforce. Well-trained workers will work faster, and with fewer mistakes, whatever their job. They will be better motivated and better prepared for promotion. Employers who do not train risk going out of business to competitors who do. Those employers who rely on poaching the employees of organisations that do train, must pay more to attract them, and deplete the pool of trained people.

The whole country needs a well-trained population. Training and education are often described to as the 'growing points' of an economy. In the UK, governments of all shades of opinion have tried to stimulate training for the past 30 years by a series of measures and initiatives. We shall look at the latest of these at the end of the week.

Commitment to training

Just going through the motions achieves nothing. To be
effective, training requires commitment from everyone
involved.

Management commitment
Employers and top managers must believe that training is
valuable for their organisation and their employees.
Managers at all levels must know what training offers for
the success of their operation. This management
commitment must also be clearly demonstrated; employees
are unlikely to take training seriously unless they have
evidence that their bosses really believe in it.

Effective methods of demonstrating management
commitment include:

Demonstrating management commitment
- A clear, positive organisational training policy
  statement
- Provision of adequate resources for training
- Regular management review of training needs, plans
  and outcomes
- Good support procedures including appraisal,
  mentoring and counselling
- Taking part in training personally at an individual and
  team level

This commitment will need continual re-affirmation; it
cannot be a once-for-all event.

Trainee commitment

Individuals must also be convinced that training is of value to them, and not just something that is only needed by others. Successful training must always change how we do things. As we have already seen, no one can force another person to develop, however good the training. To succeed, we must want to learn, believe that the training can meet our needs, and commit ourselves to success before, during and afterwards.

Not everyone welcomes the opportunity to be trained. Resistance often springs from fear. Some unskilled workers fear that to be trained will set them apart from their friends. They may be physically separated from them, asked to undertake new and harder work, appear stuck-up and stand-offish, possibly even seen as part of 'management'.

Skilled workers and professionals are more likely to resist training for reasons of pride. They may feel that they know it all already, and that to need training implies inadequacy, even that they would be demeaned by exposing their hard-won expertise to the gaze of others. They may fear that their ignorance could be displayed, and resist a situation in which their skills could be compared with that of colleagues and rivals.

Fighting against these negative pressures are many valid reasons why people may want to be trained:

Why people may want to be trained
- They have a new job
- They want a (new) job
- They want promotion
- They want to perform better
- Their job is changing
- Other people are being trained
- They want to develop as people
- It meets their long-term career objectives

The most powerful reasons for accepting training are often the long-term reasons. Many people are now making long-term plans for their careers. They will train not only for the job they hold, but the next job and even the job beyond that.

Trainer commitment
Trainers more than anyone must believe in the value of what they are doing; this is not an activity that can be undertaken successfully by the cynical or the half-hearted. There must always be an element of missionary zeal in the make-up of good trainers; after all, their job is to change people's lives for the better.

The training sequence

Three parties are directly involved in vocational training: the trainee, the trainer, and the employer or manager. To be effective, each must play their part in a sequence of five actions – what we may call the 'training sequence':

The training sequence
1 Assessing the need
2 Training design
3 Delivery
4 Use
5 Evaluation

Assessing the need

It is not enough just to have a feeling that training is 'a good thing'. The reasons why training is necessary must be established clearly. The techniques for assessing need are also relevant to evaluation, providing a 'before and after training' loop. We will look at this stage tomorrow.

Training design
There are many methods of training, from which we will have to choose carefully. This will take our time on Tuesday and Wednesday. Having chosen the methods to be used, we shall have to design the training in detail. This is particularly important if we are planning a course. This will be our subject for Thursday.

Delivery
With the planning complete, we have reached the point at which we can get on with the job. We will discuss course delivery on Friday.

Use
The training must be put into practice, or the whole exercise will have been wasted. If the training is 'on-the-job', delivery, use and evaluation will be closely combined. We will look at this on Saturday.

Evaluation
All too often, training is an act of faith. But to do the job properly, it will need evaluation; has it all been worthwhile? We shall consider ways of answering this question on Saturday.

Summary

- Training is only one method of development
- Training is much more than 'going on a course'
- Training and retraining are now essential for career and life success
- Training calls for commitment from employers, trainees and trainers
- The training sequence involves: assessing the need; training design; delivery; use, and evaluation

Assessing the need for training

Today, we will begin by considering how the need for training can be established. We will look at:

Assessing the need
- Strategic training needs
- Functional training needs
- Individual training needs
- Objective setting

Establishing the need is the first, essential stage in the training sequence, but much of what we do now will be repeated as part of the final stage – evaluation of the results of training. Indeed, this stage can only be properly completed if we can make before-and-after training comparisons, thus closing the loop.

Strategic training needs

It has been traditional to look at training needs 'bottom up'; in other words, to add together the needs of individuals and departments to make an organisation-wide plan. However, it is now often considered more effective to begin by looking at the big picture: the longer-term training needs of the whole organisation.

The starting point for this approach is the business or strategic plan of the organisation. If no such plan exists it should, for other reasons, be created. Strategic plans have human resource implications, although this is not always recognised. People with certain skills and knowledge will be needed to carry them out. It is no use planning to increase our sales by 200% if our existing sales force is stretched to the limit. We must either recruit more sales people – a costly alternative – or improve the performance of our existing force, something that demands training. It is no use

planning to introduce a new computer network, or re-equip with the latest numerically controlled machines, unless we also train everyone involved to get the best out of the equipment. If we plan to reduce rejects or improve the handling of complaints, customer service training will be imperative. Many businesses get into difficulty through neglect of this basic principle.

For success, therefore, we must examine our strategic or business plan and ask questions such as:

Strategic training planning
- Does the business or strategic plan call for additional personnel? If so, in what areas of skill? How will they be recruited?
- Does the plan require new skills or knowledge from existing personnel? If so, how will these be obtained?
- Does the plan require higher standards of job performance? If so, how will these be achieved?
- Does the plan involve major changes of product, materials, equipment, machinery, location, systems or methods? If so, what training will personnel require to implement the changes effectively?
- Does the plan call for changes of attitude and culture? If so, what are they, and how can they be achieved?

Functional training needs

Within the overall plan, we must look at the training needs of functions or departments. It may be necessary to consider the needs of everyone involved in a particular kind of work – customer contact, for example, or word processing. The need may arise for many reasons: we may have just taken over as manager; performance may be below target; the demands on the area may have increased or changed. In general, any change, whether of product, service given, methods, technology, location, manager, or individual personnel, is likely to suggest a training need.

In this situation, some form of training needs analysis will be required. 'Training Needs Analysis' (TNA) is a phrase used to describe a range of methods. At one end of the scale are highly structured techniques which are rarely used except in special situations. At the other end is informal and often purely subjective assessment.

The most effective approach in the majority of cases is a series of structured interviews with potential trainees, their managers and, if possible, their internal or external customers. The interviewing must include a representative sample of those to be trained, including all levels of performance and attitude. It is easy to get a biased picture if we talk only with the articulate, high performers or concentrate on those who have clear opinions. These interviews may be supported by inputs from the analyses of strategic or individual needs.

Questions that can be helpful in such interviews include:

Training needs analysis questions
- Which individuals, departments or groups are involved in the problem area?
- What is the reporting structure of the area?
- What work is carried out in the area?
- Do job descriptions exist, are they up to date, and what do they say?
- Who are the area's internal or external customers?
- Who initiated the survey, and why?
- Is the area, or individuals within it, failing to meet operational standards?
- If so, in what way, and what is the evidence?
- Have there been recent changes in personnel, equipment, machinery, products, location, methods or any other significant aspect? If so, what?
- Are any changes planned? If so, what?
- What previous relevant training has been given to the individuals in question?
- What skills or knowledge are lacking for efficient and effective working?
- How can these skills or knowledge be best provided?
- What standards can be set, against which the effectiveness of proposed training can be measured?

Individual training needs

There are many ways in which the training needs of individuals may surface:

Identifying individual training needs
- Tests and examinations
- Self-test instruments
- Performance appraisal
- Assessment of prior learning
- Assessment centres
- Mentoring
- Individual development planning
- Career counselling

Some of these are aimed specifically at establishing training needs; others throw up training needs as a by-product.

Tests and examinations
Formal testing and examinations are not generally used in the vocational context, but they may be incorporated in longer training courses, traineeships and apprenticeships. They are sometimes used during the recruitment and selection process. To assess training (as opposed to educational) need, tests must evaluate competence, i.e. whether the person being tested is able to carry out the task in question, as well as knowledge. Computer programming, systems analysis, shorthand and keyboard skills are amongst the areas in which objective skill testing is generally accepted.

Tests may be used in this way as an element in competence-based training such as the National Vocational Qualifications (NVQs). We will touch on these again later today, and look at the NVQ system on Saturday.

Self-test instruments
Most people love completing tests that claim to tell them about themselves. There is a magical fascination in answering a series of questions and being given a description of oneself. If the description tells us what we already know, or would fit anyone else just as closely, this never detracts from the pleasure.

Tests designed to help us establish our own training needs suffer a major drawback: it is easy to cheat. The aim of a question is usually clear, and the temptation to give the acceptable answer strong. To reduce this danger, some tests call for a questionnaire also to be completed by another person – a colleague or manager. This improves their value, but is still subjective.

Performance appraisal
Individual job performance is a key indicator of training needs. However, job performance must be regularly and fairly measured against sound standards, something that is easier in manual than in non-manual work. In non-manual areas, appraisal schemes may be used to do this, but with varying accuracy.

Appraisal may not be an effective method of assessing training needs, for a number of reasons. Many systems are poorly designed. Annual appraisal may not be frequent enough; needs should be recognised when they arise, not held over until the appraisal. Using current job performance also does not take account of training needs for possible future posts.

Appraisals are often badly carried out. Managers may be tempted to offer attendance on a course as a reward for good service, to blunt the edge of criticism, or simply as a means of rounding off the interview. They may show the appraisee a list of available courses, like a menu at a restaurant, but unless the need has already been identified, this is looking at solutions before identifying a problem. Doing this also over-emphasises course attendance as a means of training. Sending someone on a course may be the manager's attempt to overcome guilt for his poor management.

Despite these problems, appraisal systems are one of the commonest methods of establishing individual training needs, and when used properly can be effective.

Assessment of prior learning

The concept of competence is increasingly used in vocational training, and is the basis of NVQs. Competence is not 'What do they know?', but 'What can they do?' It requires both knowledge and skill, and does not depend on what books a person has read, or what courses they have attended.

The approach to competence-based qualifications begins therefore not with a course of training, but with a process aimed to establish what competences someone already has. This is known as an 'Assessment of Prior Learning' (APL). APL can be time consuming and expensive, but training needs should be clearly established.

The tools for conducting APL include:

- Briefing discussions
- Interviews
- Self-assessment instruments
- Tests and examinations
- Counselling
- Compiling a portfolio of evidence, which may include:
  - job descriptions
  - reports
  - log-books
  - cvs
  - reports
  - samples or descriptions of work
  - references

Assessment centres

Some organisations use assessment centres to produce profiles of the skills of their employees and their training needs. The centres are physical locations at which a range of assessment tools are available and to which groups are invited, for a period of two or three days. The tools are similar to those employed in APL, but may also include group exercises. Assessment centres are expensive, and for this reason most frequently used for senior personnel and those who may have potential for top management – 'high fliers'.

Mentoring

Mentors are more experienced people available to help a learner on a personal, long-term basis. Mentors can be invaluable in helping an individual to identify and find ways of meeting their training needs. We will consider their role in more detail tomorrow.

Individual career planning

Individuals who take their careers seriously may decide to produce a methodical career plan.

Career planning involves setting objectives for the type of work we wish to do, the level of responsibility we wish to have, and the kind of organisation we would like to work for. From these, we can target the experience, training and qualifications we will need. Partners, friends, managers, or professional counsellors can often help in this process.

Career planning demands maturity and cool self-analysis. But it can never be an exact science; life always holds surprises, whether pleasant – the unexpected opportunity, perhaps, or unpleasant – illness or redundancy. As we develop, our objectives are also likely to change; the parent of growing children is unlikely to have the same career objectives as the independent young graduate. Career plans need regular updating. This may be a more useful job than setting New Year resolutions.

An increasing number of individuals keep a career-long portfolio. In it will be job descriptions, samples of work, reports, references from bosses and others, certificates and other confirmations of qualifications or standards of achievement, and diaries or detailed descriptions of important phases of work or training. Such a collection is of value in the APL process, and may help when applying for jobs.

Career counselling
Increasing use is now made of counselling in planning careers or dealing with career problems. It is especially appropriate at career crossroads; initial choice of vocation, mid-career crises and plateauing, and when preparing for retirement. We should not think of counselling as of help only to those who have lost their job; it can be helpful to anyone who wishes to get the best from their career. Counselling will usually throw up needs for training, and if it has been thorough, the results are likely to be very accurate.

Objective setting

Having established a need for training, we must set objectives for that training. Clear objectives will help us to choose the best way of meeting the need and to evaluate the results. (We shall meet objectives again during training design. The objectives we are now discussing are for individual trainees or for groups of trainees with similar needs.)

Objective setting involves both trainees and their managers. It is vital that they agree in advance what the objectives of the training are, how achievement of them is to be assessed, and how the new skills and knowledge will be used. If both are involved at this stage, they will feel commitment to the later stages, and monitoring progress will be easy and natural. It can be helpful to draw up objectives in the form of a contract between trainee, manager and trainer; we will look at such 'training contracts' a little later.

Training objectives do not need to be complex. If our analysis of needs has been effective, there may be little more to do but write down the result systematically.

Training objectives should be:

- Clearly defined
- Measurable whenever possible
- Realistic
- Expressed in behavioural terms, i.e. what the trainee will be able to do after training.

Writing the objectives down and providing copies for everyone concerned is a helpful discipline.

Here is a typical list of training objectives.

For an intake of newly recruited graduates:

1994 Graduate intake – training objectives

By the end of training, each member of the intake will:
- Know the structure of the organisation and have met the senior personnel
- Be familiar with the current range of products
- Know the marketing strategy and the principle categories of customer
- Of the department to which they are allocated, have:
  - met and established good relationships with the personnel
  - learnt the procedures and methods
  - settled into their own position

Target date: four months after joining

Training contracts

A 'training contract' is an agreement drawn up between an individual learner and his or her boss. A third party, such as the training manager or a mentor, may also be involved. Under the terms of the agreement, each party accepts specified responsibilities. Learners will agree to use their best endeavours to gain certain skills, knowledge or qualifications; the boss will agree to allow the necessary time and facilities; the mentor or other trainer will agree to provide support, advice and counselling. To work well, such a contract must be specific in its detail, including the targets, methods of assessment and timescale.

A typical training contract is shown opposite.

TRAINING CONTRACT

Parties to the contract: John Smith, Supervisor
Mary Brown, Dept. Manager
Tom Sawyer, Training Officer

Aim: For John Smith to become fully skilled in the operation of the 'Skyhy' stock control system

John Smith will:
- Read and become familiar with the system manual
- Take every opportunity to use the system in the course of his normal duties
- Raise any queries with Mary

Mary Brown will:
- Allow John use of his computer terminal whenever practicable
- Channel as many appropriate stock enquiries to John as possible
- Allow John as much time off other duties as the demands of the department's work allow to learn the system
- Set aside 30 minutes each Friday afternoon to discuss progress with John, and to answer queries
- Make available any additional time or facilities necessary to ensure John achieves his target

Tom Sawyer will: Coach John as necessary to help his understanding

Summary

- Training needs should be assessed methodically at strategic, functional and individual level
- Strategic training needs are derived from the business or strategic plan
- Functional training needs may be established by training needs analysis, which is usually conducted by a series of structured interviews
- Individual training needs may be established by a wide range of methods including: tests and examinations, self-test instruments, performance appraisal, the assessment of prior learning, assessment centres, mentoring, individual development planning and career counselling
- Clear objectives should be set for training
- Training 'contracts' can help in some situations

Choice of method: requirements for effective training

Today we will take a first look at the second step of the training sequence: training design. We will start to consider our choice of training method:

Choice of method
- Finance
- Time
- The trainer(s)
- Accommodation and equipment
- The trainee(s)
- What is to be learnt
- On- and off-the-job training

There is a danger that, in setting up training, we may follow tradition blindly. Previous methods (if there have been any) may be the best, but we should always consider alternatives.

Training requires resources of money, time and effort and we must make the best use of what is available.

Finance

Training is not an area in which it is sensible to shop by price. It is equally wrong to assume the most expensive must be the best, or that cheap solutions will be adequate to meet our needs. The costs can be very different for different methods of training aimed at the same objectives. The only cost of on-the-job coaching, for example, may be marginal managerial time. An off-the-job course covering the same area may involve fees, trainee travel and subsistence and the trainee's wages while on the course. The choice will depend on the individual circumstances; there is no short cut to a proper appraisal of whatever methods are on offer.

The complete costs of training may include:

- Tuition and examination fees
- Books, software, films and other material
- Training facility and equipment costs; room and equipment hire etc.
- Trainers'/consultants' fees and expenses
- Trainees' travel and subsistence expenses
- Trainees' wages/salary costs, or costs of lost production
- Training and personnel department and other administrative costs and overheads
- Management, mentoring or tutoring costs and overheads

Grants may be available to help offset training costs. The best source of information on these is our local TEC or LEC. (These are discussed on Saturday.)

When we have made our choice of training method, we shall need, like all good managers, to set a budget.

Time

Time may be important in several ways. Induction training of employees into a new post is always subject to time pressure; it is in everyone's interests to make the 'learning curve' as steep as possible. There may be deadlines by which the training must be complete: the installation of new equipment, for example, the launch of a new product, or the opening of new premises.

There is often felt to be a limit to the amount of time for which trainees can be spared from a busy post. Even when training is agreed to be essential, managers may be reluctant to give their people adequate time to undergo it. If the benefits are less clear-cut or immediate (e.g. for supervisory training), this reluctance is often much stronger.

Training which is planned to take place over a lengthy period, on-the-job, for example, or by regular day release, may be made difficult by unplanned alterations to the trainee's situation; a job move, or the attitude of a new boss.

Realism is essential; there is nothing to be gained by choosing training methods which demand time that cannot be spared.

The trainers

Training may be provided by a range of people. Some of the methods we will look at today can only be supplied by one kind of provider; for some there is a choice. Possible providers of training include:

- In-house training professionals
- External consultants
- Local colleges
- Professional bodies
- Managers
- Colleagues

One of the key choices is often whether to appoint in-house training professionals or rely on outside resources. There has been a tendency in recent years to slim down training departments and close apprentice training schools. Many organisations use both, engaging outsiders for more specialised requirements such as management training.

A few training consultants seek to persuade clients that their methods contain unique ingredients, rather like patent medicines. However, like patent medicines, these ingredients are often given impressive names or acronyms which mean little or nothing. In practice, the match between a consultant's experience and our own environment is often the key factor in making a successful choice.

If we use internal trainers it is essential that they have themselves been properly trained for the use we make of them. This may become a problem when managers and colleagues are used to train, as in several of the methods we will look at tomorrow. There is a wide range of training available for coaches, mentors and course leaders. In the UK, the Training and Development Lead Body (TDLB) has laid down standards of competence for National Vocational Qualifications (NVQs) for trainers at various levels.

Accommodation and equipment

Virtually all training methods require specialised accommodation and equipment of some kind. Even the simplest course will require an appropriate training area with suitable furniture and basic equipment.

The environment must be suitable for the use we intend. The layout of the teaching room can have a big effect on the efficiency of training. If it is laid out as a classroom, for example, it will be hard to generate a participative atmosphere. If everyone cannot see and hear properly, our efforts will be wasted. The noise and temperature levels must be comfortable, and there must be protection from distractions. Our chosen methods may require rooms for group activities or individual study. Catering facilities must be appropriate.

Most off-the-job training methods will require a minimum level of equipment; flipcharts, markers, overhead projector (ohp) and screen. We may need 35mm slide projectors, video equipment (with or without camcorder and large screen), or film projector and screen. We may need demonstration machinery, models or mock-ups. At the extreme end of the scale, our training methods may call for complex and costly equipment such as a language laboratory or a simulator. Training frequently benefits from the support of a good library or information centre.

The trainee(s)

The training must be tailored to the people who are to be trained. Training suitable for a group of experienced, time-served machinists, for example, would not help a group of individuals straight from the nearest Job Centre, or vice versa. The aspects of trainees that we must consider in choosing training methods include:

Analysing trainees
- How many are there?
- What is their general level of education?
- What relevant qualifications do they already have?
- What experience have they had?
- Why have they been chosen for training?
- What jobs (if any) do they now do?
- Why should they want to be trained?
- Do they work together as a team?

We must be clear whether we are choosing training methods for an individual, a small or large group, a continuing stream of trainees (e.g. induction training for new starters), or occasional but repeated batches (e.g. apprentices or graduates).

Team training

If our aim really is to lead a team, as opposed to a collection of individuals, we must train as a team. This will, by definition, involve group activities. In many cases, the most appropriate training will be in-house training courses centred on the key activities of the team. This may be supplemented by training targeted specifically at developing the interpersonal elements of the team work, possibly involving role-playing and sensitivity training of various kinds. One method used for this is adventure training, which we will look at tomorrow.

What is to be learnt

Learning can cover three broad areas: knowledge, skills or attitudes. There are few learning activities which do not involve all three. Thus, a passing a written examination demands not only the acquisition of knowledge, but also the skill to organise and display that knowledge to satisfy the examiner, and the strong motivation to keep us going.

The emphasis in training is usually on the development skills: driving an HGV, for example; using a particular computer software package; or giving an effective presentation. The same is true of many ingredients in management training. It is not possible to develop skill without practice and feedback over an appropriate length of time which may be weeks or months. Our choice of training method must take this into account.

Attitude change is an important ingredient in many kinds of training, such as customer care and team building. This may not require the long periods of time needed to develop skills, but does call for continuing follow-up, support and monitoring in the working environment.

On- or off-the-job training?

Training methods are often split between on- and off-the job, although several methods involve both. As the name suggests, on-the-job training is carried out while trainees are at their normal place of work and doing, as far as practicable, the work for which they are paid. Off-the-job training, on the other hand, takes place in a special location (a classroom or training centre, for example) and does not include productive work.

Learning by doing is the most natural form of training. Few instructors would attempt to teach driving or swimming, for example, in a classroom. On-the-job training has many advantages. It does not require its own facilities, equipment or trainer, and is thus often cheaper than off-the-job training. Behaviour is learnt in the workplace, and does not need transferring.

However, on-the-job training has drawbacks. It requires one-to-one contact, which can demand much of the trainer's time. It is harder to structure and control; it can feel rather untidy. There are often distractions to the trainee, and trainees may themselves prove a distraction to others. If productive work is done by the trainee, there may be pressure to achieve targets; if team-working is involved, the trainee will be a weak link. If there is direct contact with customers, the level of service may suffer. There may be safety problems. The training restaurant, the training hospital or the hair salon can offer the best of both worlds, but in other occupations the combination may be harder to achieve.

Some managers feel that on-the-job training is second best. Others may hope that by giving someone else the responsibility, they can get it off their plate, but, as a manager, this is something we must never seek to do. Effective training usually requires both on- and off-the-job elements. Where knowledge is important, it is best acquired in the classroom or the study. Where skills must be developed, there must be practice on the job.

Summary

- There are several important factors which must be taken into account in designing training
- The costs of different methods must be assessed and compared
- Trainees and their managers must be prepared to allocate the necessary time
- The choice of trainers can be crucial
- Suitable accommodation and equipment must be provided
- The characteristics of the trainees must be analysed, as individuals and as a group
- The mix of knowledge, skills and attitudes to be learnt must be established
- The choice between on- and off-the-job training is important; a mix of the two may be most effective

Choice of method II: types of training method

We will now look at some of the principal methods of training. We shall look in detail at:

Training methods
- On-the-job training
- Off-the-job training
- New employee training

On-the-job training

On-the-job training can be carried out using many methods, most of which are an extension of the principles of good management.

Leadership and example
Looking back on their career, many people would agree that the periods in which they learnt most were those in which they worked for a good boss. Good bosses are in loco parentis to those who work for them and will guide, set objectives, motivate, advise, support, correct and, if necessary, discipline. Just as children learn, often unconsciously, from parents, so workers learn, unconsciously, from their boss. Attitudes such as honesty, openness, and commitment to the organisation and its customers rub off. These factors make a powerful training package; the boss has a central role.

Coaching

Coaching is at the heart of on-the-job training.
Demonstration followed by practice and feedback is the
most natural method of learning any skill, whether, for
example, operating machinery, using a clerical procedure, or
negotiating with a supplier. All on-the-job training, by
whatever method, must include an element of coaching.

All good bosses coach their people. From the day new
employees walk through the door, the boss will have the
prime responsibility to explain what is expected of them, the
standards against which they will be judged, and how they
can get help. The responsibility for coaching lies with the
boss, but like other tasks it can, and in many cases should be
delegated. The best person to delegate coaching to is Nellie.
No one knows who the first Nellie was, but it is 'next to
Nellie' that people learn best on-the-job. Nellies must have
certain characteristics and must:

Effective coaches
- be experienced in the job
- be free from bad and unsafe working habits
- be articulate in explanation
- be patient with learners
- have adequate time to devote to the learner
- be sufficiently secure not to feel threatened by
  learners who may surpass their own skills

Whether done by Nellie or her boss, effective coaching will
need to follow certain guidelines and must:

Effective coaching

- Demonstrate
- Analyse and explain
- Encourage the trainee to make their own attempts and experiments without interference (unless safety is at stake)
- Set targets for progress
- Be available to answer queries and give help when asked
- Give meaningful feedback and encouragement at appropriate intervals
- Review and reset targets as progress is made
- Obtain additional help if needed

Mentoring

Mentoring is the continuing, personal support of a learner by someone who is not his or her boss. It is based on counselling, and supports learners and helps them to develop their own approach and solutions to problems. Mentors are usually more experienced workers, but unlike tutors their role is not as a subject expert. The absence of a boss–subordinate relationship removes threat.

Mentoring usually takes the form of a series of meetings, which may be regular (e.g. once a month) or ad hoc (e.g. when difficulties are encountered). The meetings are usually on a one-to-one basis, as the confidential, personal relationship between mentor and learner is important for success. However, mentor groups including more than one learner in a similar situation may sometimes be practicable.

Delegation

Delegation is essential to good management. It is also a powerful training technique. Managers who hand a job that they could do themselves to subordinates, offer them an opportunity to develop new skills and the confidence to use them.

Effective delegation is one of the hardest things for a manager to learn. Most managers are promoted to their posts because they have demonstrated their ability to carry out the work in their area well; as managers, they must learn to get others to do it instead.

Here are some guidelines for successful delegation:

Successful delegation
- Explain why we are delegating, and why we have chosen that individual
- Say what the objectives of the task are
- Clarify how success will be measured
- List what resources may be used, and how they can be obtained
- Make clear that we are available if needed, but will otherwise not interfere

And then
- Stand well back
- Help the subordinate to overcome any problems if they call for our help
- Give supportive feedback when the task is complete

Job rotation
Encouraging jobholders to move from one job to another in the same grade can be an excellent training method. It offers new skills, helps flexibility of working, and can freshen stale motivation. It is especially helpful in broadening the

experience of younger people and offering new challenges to older workers for whom promotion is not available. To provide effective training, the following steps must be taken:

Successful job rotation
- The objectives must be explained to and accepted by both jobholders
- Each must be given a full induction, preferably by the existing jobholder
- Continuing support and interest must be shown by the manager
- The opportunity to revert to the original situation must be available

Job enrichment and multi-skilling
'Job enrichment' is the technique of adding elements or responsibilities to a job to make it more satisfying to the jobholder. The opportunity may be given, for example, to see jobs through from start to finish, to make direct contact with customers, or make changes to the product design to overcome problems in manufacture or use.

'Multi-skilling' is providing the opportunity and the training for workers to operate in a range of jobs. In some organisations, the range is very wide and includes what have previously been thought of as both manual and non-manual work: machining, selling the product, and chasing non-payers, for example.

Whilst job enrichment And multi-skilling are not, in themselves, training techniques, both can provide powerful development.

Secondment and attachment
Seconding or attaching people to an area or department
other than their own can be an effective form of training.
Thus salespeople or designers may spend time in the
production area, or computer staff in, say, the accounts
department. Such periods can develop new skills and
knowledge, and broaden trainees' understanding of the
work they already do.

As with other training methods, secondment requires
briefing of the trainee before it is undertaken, and support
and follow-up afterwards.

Special assignments and action learning
'Action learning' involves trainees undertaking special
assignments, usually in a different organisation or
environment from their own. Their work is supported by a
tutor group of other trainees, with a facilitator or mentor, in
which progress and problems can be discussed. The
technique is most commonly used for senior management
trainees, but can be adapted to other situations. Action
learning calls for:

Successful action learning
- An assignment which is challenging, relevant and
  achievable
- Firm mentor support
- A good, well-matched, tutorial group
- A real opportunity for implementation

Work-shadowing

Observing an experienced worker at work can be helpful. It is sometimes used for those likely to be promoted to managerial posts, and for school-children wishing to learn about particular careers. Unfortunately, few people can work normally whilst they are being closely watched for long periods. It is also rare for the person being shadowed to have the time, skill and interest to explain their actions.

'Cook's tours'

A sequence of visits to observe the work of different departments can help in induction, graduate training and other situations. It can develop personal contacts, and show the inter-relationships between areas and functions.

Tours should be preceded by a discussion between trainees and their manager about the objectives to be achieved, the points to be looked out for, and the key people to get to know. They must allow an appropriate amount of time in each area; too short and there is no time to build relationships, pick up the feel of an area, and ask questions; too long and both trainee and departmental staff may find it burdensome. It is helpful for trainees to record their experience in a diary or prepare a more formal report. Debriefing by the manager is essential.

Off-the-job training

Off-the-job training frequently takes the form of courses. Courses may be of any length, from an hour or two to many months. It is useful to divide courses into 'long' and 'short'; 'long' can be thought of as those of more than a week's duration, and 'short' those of a week or less.

Other words for such events include: 'workshops', 'seminars' and 'training events'.

Short courses

For many people the very word 'training' conjures up the picture of a dozen people sitting in a horse-shoe shaped group, listening to someone lecturing with the aid of an overhead projector. Such courses are run by an enormous range of organisations on an almost endless variety of subjects. They are the backbone of the training provided by professional organisations and training consultancies. They are a common format for the work of company training departments and a frequent ingredient in the industrial training curricula of local colleges.

'Public' or 'open' courses are offered to all comers who are prepared to pay the fees. 'In-company' or 'in-house' courses are mounted for chosen members of an organisation. Each have their characteristic advantages and disadvantages:

Public short courses

Advantages
- Participants mix with and learn from those of other organisations
- Individuals are readily catered for
- Individuals may feel less threat than when training with colleagues

Disadvantages
- The unit cost can be expensive
- There may be a long wait for a suitable course
- Methods and skills learnt may not match the needs of every organisation

In-house short courses

Advantages
- They may be tailored to meet specific needs
- They can be arranged for suitable times and locations
- Working teams can train together
- Unit cost will be lower than public courses

Disadvantages
- They require a group to be released at the same time
- Training with colleagues may present a threat

Long courses, day and block release

Long off-the-job courses are traditionally used for management, computer programmers and systems analysts and other specialist training.

Regular 'day release' or periods of 'block release' are frequently included in college courses for a variety of qualifications. As the name implies, day release involves trainees attending a college or similar regularly for off-the-job training, often once a week. Block release involves training for several weeks continuously, alternating with on-the-job practical learning. Similar periods of college-based learning are incorporated into the 'sandwich' format of degree and diploma courses. In these, off-the-job periods may be as little as three months, or may last for a complete, three-term, academic year.

The advantages and disadvantages of long courses include:

Advantages
- Complete detachment from the work situation and its pressures
- Scope for major learning and re-learning
- Can provide powerful interpersonal experiences
- Reinforcement of learning by the use of a range of techniques

Disadvantages
- Remote from working context
- Inflexible in matching individual needs
- Problems in re-entry and transfer of learning to the real world

Private reading
It ill behoves an author to play down the value of private reading. There has never been a greater range of books on

vocational subjects than there is today. Many of them, like the one you are now reading, are precisely targeted at areas of need, carefully planned, and brilliantly executed. Those reading them cannot help but benefit.

Books apart, there is now also a wide selection of professional journals and magazines specialising in vocational subjects. These have the advantage over even the very best books in that they are fully up to date. Most people would benefit from a subscription to at least one such periodical.

However, reading can by itself do little to improve skills, and must be supported by practice and the other aids to skill development.

Distance learning
'Distance learning' can describe any situation in which learner and teacher are remote from each other. It thus describes traditional correspondence courses, in which learning material and students' exercises are exchanged by

post. In recent years, such courses have been enhanced by the addition of other learning media such as audio- and video-tapes and, most recently, cd-rom. Longer courses are frequently supported by periods of face-to-face tuition at weekend or longer schools. In the UK, the growth of the Open University and Open Colleges has done much to strengthen this movement.

The most recent developments link distance-learning methods to practical skills development by requiring the learner to practise their new skills in their working situation. This process is supported and monitored by keeping a diary or portfolio, collecting evidence of achievement (e.g. working reports, manager's comments etc.), and mentoring.

Distance learning and 'open learning' are sometimes confused. 'Open learning' is a term used to describe courses, usually leading to qualifications, which do not have limiting entry requirements. The courses of the Open University are thus both 'distance' and 'open' learning.

Programmed learning and computer-based training
Knowledge and some skills may be developed by the use of programmed learning. Programmes may be supplied in book form, as hard copy for 'learning machines' (now obsolete), disks for micros, or cd-roms.

The value of both books and micro disks is limited. In practice, the latter are no more than a text on a screen rather than on a page. The questions are limited to multiple-choice ones and the branching logic has limited value. Programmes based on cd-rom (compact disks – read-only memory, which can be used with PCs equipped with the special drives) are far more powerful. They include features such as complex choices, still and moving graphics, and sound etc. that enable them to be truly interactive and respond to the learner's needs as learning proceeds.

Simulation
Simulation has been developed as a powerful training technique for certain skills. The simulator creates an environment (e.g. the flight-deck or the locomotive cab) in which the trainee experiences as closely as possible the same sensations as in real life. These may include sights, sounds, physical movement and indications on the control panel. To justify the substantial capital costs of simulators, the throughput of trainees and the costs and risks of real-life training must be high.

The growth of the techniques of 'virtual reality' may extend the range of situations in which simulation is useful. With virtual reality, individuals using the equipment (which may include special visors, helmets, gloves etc.) experience many of the sensations that their actions would produce in the real world.

Adventure training
'Adventure training' has developed from work in the armed forces, and the original Outward Bound schools designed primarily for young people. The technique involves a period of several days – typically a week – in which a group is invited to undertake a range of outdoor activities, either as individuals, in small groups, or as a larger team.

The activities are usually of a physically demanding nature: abseiling, rock-climbing, orienteering, white-water canoeing, back-packing across rough country, surmounting obstacles with burdens, etc. The activities aim to give the trainees a variety of benefits which typically include increased individual confidence and maturity, better team working and interdependence skills, or enhanced leadership skills.

By definition, such training is not without physical risks, and its value is open to debate. For some, it is a powerful training tool; for others it offers nothing more than an unusual thrill and a lot of muddy boots. Its critics feel that the problems of transfer from training to the work situation are particularly difficult.

Community activities
Community activities include office-holding in clubs and societies, voluntary services of all kinds, magistrates' duties and membership of local councils. The attitude of employers to these vary, but some see them as a valuable form of training.

Such activities often provide satisfactions and outlets that the working environment may not. They also, in many cases, call for different skills. Whether such skills are easily transferred to the working environment is doubtful. In many cases the individual may, consciously or unconsciously, build a Chinese wall between the two worlds.

New employee training

We saw yesterday that one factor in the choice of training methods is the numbers to be trained, and whether the needs are regular and repeated over time. The commonest repeated group needs are those associated with new employees in an organisation; apprenticeships, graduate training and induction training.

Apprenticeships

Apprenticeships are the oldest recorded method of industrial training, and have been used for at least 600 years. An apprentice is contracted to a period of training lasting a set number of years – anything from three to seven. Typical apprentice programmes include:

- Off-the-job training in basic skills, usually in an apprentice training school
- Supervised, on-the-job experience
- Mentoring by an experienced worker
- Theoretical education by day or block release

Apprenticeships are most strongly associated with manual craft skills, but have also been used for what are now regarded as professional jobs, such as a barrister or an accountant.

Unfortunately, apprenticeships have become associated with restrictive practices by trade unions and professional bodies, aimed to add scarcity value to skilled labour. Arbitrary age limits have also made entry difficult. Some employers have used apprenticeships as a source of cheap labour. Others have failed to train for the skills they need, relying on poaching skilled labour others. The length of apprenticeships makes forecasting the requirements for skilled labour difficult.

Despite these problems, the combination of on- and off-the-job learning, skill and theory, and the coaching relationship with a skilled practitioner can provide an ideal balance of training.

Recently, governments within the UK have attempted to develop various forms of youth training to replace or supplement apprenticeships. These have been subject to political pressures and their success is generally felt to have been limited. However, they do offer the opportunity for those leaving school at the minimum age to receive training and the chance of a full-time job.

Induction training
The effective training of new recruits in an organisation is of great importance. It is crucial for those beginning their career; their first experiences of the world of work are as significant for their later development as the early experiences of childhood.

Induction is also necessary for those moving or being promoted to a new post within their existing organisation, an aspect of training that may be forgotten. It is most often neglected when someone is promoted for the first time into a post with supervisory or management responsibilities. It is assumed that, because someone is a brilliant classroom teacher, for example, they must make a good head of department, or that a fine designer must make a good engineering manager. But management has its own skills which call for careful training.

The elements in a systematic induction package include:

- Basic facts about the organisation
- The recruit's department/work area
- The recruit's job
- Housekeeping and safety
- Training and development opportunities
- Basic conditions of employment

Graduate training
The training of graduates, whilst not strictly different from other kinds of induction training, has its own patterns and problems. There are few problems where the trainee's degree is clearly vocational (e.g. accounting, law, mechanical engineering, etc.). Such graduates may be recruited direct into operational posts. The problems arise when graduates with non-vocational degrees (history, geography, English, sociology etc.) are recruited.

These problems are compounded by the traditional view of graduates as management trainees. This view is untenable (except for a very small minority) at the now greatly increased annual output of graduates; there simply aren't enough top jobs to go round!

Graduates with non-vocational degrees who are not recruited as management trainees need to develop realistic job skills, attitudes and expectations. The traditional 'cook's tours' (see p. 50) may not help. The need will be for planned on- and off-the-job training in the appropriate skill areas, support and encouragement to study for formal vocational qualifications, and, above all, sound mentoring.

Summary

- There is a very wide range of training methods; we should consider them all
- On-the-job training methods include: leadership and example, coaching, mentoring, delegation, job rotation, job enrichment and multi-skilling, secondment and attachment, special assignments and action learning, work shadowing and 'cook's tours'
- Off-the-job training methods include: courses, which may be short, long, by day or block release, and public or in-company; private reading; distance learning; programmed and computer-based learning, including simulation; adventure training; and community activities
- New starter training includes: apprenticeships, induction packages and various approaches to graduate training

Designing a training course

We will now assume that we decided, yesterday, that a short off-the-job course was the method that would meet our needs best. Today and tomorrow we will concentrate on such a course; designing it today, and delivering it tomorrow. We will look at:

Course design
- The psychology of learning
- Content
- Delivery methods
- The timetable

The psychology of learning

Before looking at the practical details of our event, it will help to spend a few minutes considering theory. Learning, whether knowledge, skills or changed behaviour, will best take place under certain conditions. These include:

- Positive motivation
- A familiar starting point
- Meaningfulness
- Insight
- Reinforcement

It is also useful to look at the differences between adults and children as trainees.

Positive motivation
Strong, positive motivation is virtually essential to learning. However, even if positive motivators are present, there may be barriers to learning.

A familiar starting point
Learners must start from somewhere familiar; the lesson must connect with something they already know. This is difficult in a group with widely different backgrounds or levels of skill. As trainers, we must learn as much as possible about our potential trainees early in the design process.

It is usually better to work from the concrete to abstract. Most people prefer starting from a situation, experience or example rather than a theory.

Meaningfulness
Learning should seem meaningful to the learner. Compare, for example, being asked to learn the actions necessary to thread a needle or change a car wheel to learning a

meaningless sequence of movements; or learning a poem or a set of fire instructions, to learning a list of nonsense syllables.

The difficulty, in practice, is that what makes sense to one learner may sound like nonsense to another. A blackboard full of mathematical formulae will be meaningless to non-mathematicians, and passages in an unknown language to non-linguists. It is essential that we know how much our participants already know.

Insight

Insight into the new and unfamiliar can require much effort from both learner and teacher. It may be a skill, such as how to play a tricky piano passage or land an aircraft safely; or understanding, perhaps, a new theorem in geometry or the function of a complex valve; or behaviour, such as listening effectively to a candidate at a selection interview or restraining the urge to cause-jump when problem-solving.

An explanation, demonstration or example which helps one learner, may do nothing for another. Apart from differing backgrounds, individuals think in different ways; some use pictures, others sounds, and yet others touch and feeling. We must provide material that will help all.

Reinforcement

There are few occasions in which the first attempt at something new is successful. All learning needs reinforcement, and this can be given in a number of ways.

Success is a strong reinforcer. If we achieve the result we want, we will be motivated to repeat what we have done, but it is essential that we know when we have succeeded. A systematic mixture of reward and punishment can provide powerful reinforcement, but can be difficult to set up for adult trainees. The easiest reward to give is praise, but this must be genuine and acceptable. The most usual form of punishment is criticism, although it may also demotivate the trainee and is a dangerous weapon. For all these reinforcers, trainees must receive feedback; we shall look at this tomorrow.

Rote learning can help, as with a multiplication table, a poem, a tennis stroke or whatever. However, adults do not usually respond well in public to an approach which reminds them of school-days. Practice by itself is in any case not enough; mistakes must be corrected.

Adults as trainees
Adults approach learning in a different frame of mind from children. A style that suits children will cause resentment and resistance in adults; they may reject both us and the training we offer. Adults have amassed their own experience; they are less likely than children to accept

second-hand experience without question. Adults are more concerned than children with the 'bottom line' of the training; i.e., what value will it be to them in the foreseeable future? Above all, adults will not hesitate to challenge the authority of their teachers. It is not enough to say to a group of adults, 'Believe this because I say it is true.'

Some people even regard the training situation as a threat to their self respect, and take every opportunity to dispute what they are told. Handling a group that contains such a trainee is a demanding situation, and can become destructive.

Content

The subject matter to be covered is the natural starting point of the design phase for our course. But before entering into the detail of what must be learnt, we must define the objectives.

Objectives
We discussed objectives on Tuesday, when we considered setting training objectives for individuals or for groups with the same needs. We must now set objectives for the course we are designing. The individual objectives of every participant must match at least some of the course objectives; if not, they should not have been selected to attend. The needs of some groups (an intake of new employees, for example, or a department learning to use new equipment) are virtually identical. For other groups (such as those on public courses), it is difficult to set objectives that will cover more than a proportion of the objectives of each individual.

The guidelines for writing individual objectives (see Tuesday, p 38) will also help in writing course objectives. Here is a set of objectives for a two-day workshop in public speaking and presentation:

Effective presentation workshop objectives
By the end of the workshop, participants will :
* Know how to prepare for a presentation
* Know the main dos and don'ts for giving a successful speech
* Have practised giving a presentation
* Have received feedback and advice
* Have prepared an action plan for continued improvement

Course content

If, as a consultant or an in-house trainer, we are designing a course to meet the needs of a group, a needs analysis will be the best starting point. If we are designing a public course, or a course to be generally available, we will begin from whatever indications of need (or of the market, which may not be the same thing) we have.

The detailed content must be filled in during course preparation, using existing material or creating new.

Existing material

Previously used material can be a great help; all trainers use it. It may be our own, from a previous event, produced by a colleague, licensed by another training organisation or picked up along the way from some long-forgotten source.

Some trainers have reduced plagiary to a fine art. But there is a balance to be struck. Whilst we would be silly not to use any legitimate source of help, using existing material without further thought can be dangerous:

The dangers of existing material
- It may have been prepared for a different industry/ kind of trainee – case-studies etc. may be irrelevant
- It may be out of date
- It may be stale
- It may not have worked well last time
- It may be collected from so many sources it is disjointed and incoherent
- It may be too obviously from the US (where much training material originates)
- It may be copyright material

In any case, we would be wise to brush up our knowledge before leading a course. To take material off the shelf without other preparation is a temptation we must resist.

New material

Some trainers pride themselves on their ability to lead training events in virtually any subject, however small their own direct knowledge. Trainers who adopt this approach rely on two resources: their ability to research a subject quickly and efficiently, and their ability to unlock the knowledge and experience of the trainees they are working with. But moral obligations apart, trainees have a knack of probing trainers' weaknesses. To brush up on the latest thinking, or fill in the corners of a subject is one thing; to pretend we are experts in a field we hardly know will only bring us and training in general into disrepute.

If we do decide to create new material, we must search for illustrations and examples from what we have done and seen ourselves. Our training will be more powerful and convincing if we enrich it with our direct experiences and first-hand knowledge.

Delivery methods

There is a massive range of methods of delivery; over 300 have been identified, although many of these overlap or have only specialised application. Our choice of delivery method will depend on a number of factors, including:

- The subject area to be covered
- The characteristics of the trainees
- Group size
- Time available
- Facilities available
- Trainers' skills

The most commonly used methods include:

- Lectures
- Group discussion
- Case-studies
- Questionnaires
- Role-playing
- Demonstration and practice
- In-tray exercises
- Films/videos
- Games
- Handouts

We will look at hints for the successful use of the main methods tomorrow.

Lectures
Lectures are a trap for inexperienced trainers. They give the feeling that knowledge has been transferred. But as anyone who has subjected trainees to an examination after a lecture (especially a week or more afterwards) will have found out, transfer of knowledge is extremely limited. Lecturing is also a poor technique for improving understanding, almost

useless for developing skills and can even be counter-productive for changing attitudes. 'Don't lecture me!' is a common reaction.

We will often need to offer input during training, on the processes, content and by way of feedback. But we must do it in short bursts. If we feel we must go on for longer than about 20 minutes, we should add other methods, such as group discussion.

Group discussion
Group discussion has great value during training. For the trainer, it gives information about the interests, existing knowledge and problems of the trainees and is thus particularly useful near the start of a course. Discussion motivates trainees by involving them and giving them the opportunity to air their views. It also helps to clarify and reinforce thinking by getting to grips with a new subject or an unfamiliar angle. Discussion may also add to or even correct the trainer's material; we must be prepared to accept this possibility humbly.

Case-studies
Case-studies are learning exercises based on real-life or fictional circumstances. They can be of any length or degree of complexity, from work for an hour to many weeks. They may be designed for individual, group or whole-course use.

Case-studies are usually presented in the form of a written brief given to participants, although the briefing may, for special reasons (such as the development of listening or questioning skills) be given orally. All participants may be given an identical brief, or briefs may deliberately vary in order to set up a problem-solving or conflict-resolution situation. Briefs may contain only partial information, leaving participants to fill in the gaps in various ways. Trainees may be expected to role-play as one of a number of participants in a situation, with a particular interest or sphere of responsibility.

Case-studies must be suitable for the background of the trainees; a case-study in forestry, for example, is unlikely to go down well with a group of mechanical engineers. On the other hand, an engineering case-study must be factually correct, or will certainly produce cries of 'That isn't how we do it!'

Case-studies must illustrate the ground to be covered without irrelevant material. They must contain all the necessary facts, and those facts must be beyond challenge. They must be up to date in every way, especially technologically and legislatively. They must provide interest and challenges appropriate for the group, but be capable of resolution within the time and using the other resources available. Like a good story, they must have a clear, credible ending. If they are drawn from real life, information on what actually happened must be available, ideally from someone who was involved.

We may develop our own case-studies, or use those that have been prepared by others. There are several libraries of ready-prepared case-studies. Normally use is subject to licence and payment of a fee.

Questionnaires

Self-completion questionnaires (sometimes called 'instruments') have a variety of uses in training. They can focus trainees' thinking on a particular area, give insight and awareness of a need, generate and give a framework for discussion, and can test and demonstrate progress.

There are numerous ready-made questionnaires, and it is not difficult to tailor-make our own. However, it is essential that the results can be interpreted to trainees' satisfaction, and this may require careful testing with suitable groups. If factual answers are called for, they must be available and totally accurate.

Role-playing

Asking trainees to act out certain roles (e.g. a dissatisfied customer, a trade union negotiator etc.) can form a useful technique in many kinds of training. It is of great value in training aimed at developing interpersonal skills: interviewing, appraisal, discipline, customer service, negotiation etc. There may be value in role-reversal, i.e. asking junior staff to act the role of managers, company negotiators that of trade union officials, customer service staff that of complaining customers etc.

Role-playing exercises are usually conducted in front of the group, who are then asked to give feedback. Video recording may also be used with good effect. Participants must be well briefed in advance, and for more complex exercises (e.g. selection interviewing) they will need plenty of time for preparation. The way in which feedback is given is also important; we will think about this tomorrow.

The use of role-playing is common in training in interpersonal skills (e.g. interviewing techniques). However, it is harder for a trainer to demonstrate 'correct' methods (e.g. of reprimanding a subordinate) and this may be better done with the use of a suitable video or film.

Demonstration and practice
We discussed the effectiveness of coaching as a training technique yesterday. As it requires one-to-one attention, application to off-the-job courses may be difficult. However, this can sometimes be overcome by using trainees to observe and criticise each other. Whilst the quality of feedback may be lower, the role of observer can give additional insights to trainees; active observation is an efficient teacher.

In-tray exercises
A classic management training technique (also occasionally used as part of a selection or assessment process) is to face the trainee with an in-tray containing numerous documents, and ask for their response to each. Letters, faxes, internal memos etc. must be read, evaluated and either acted upon with an appropriate degree of priority, or ignored. The exercise can be conducted by teams or individuals, and either observed or evaluated subsequently on paper. It can be incorporated into a competitive game; this technique is discussed a little later.

Videos/films
Videos (which are more convenient to use for smaller
groups) and films are widely used for many kinds of
training. They offer a number of advantages, but also,
however, have a number of drawbacks. They may not,
therefore, be the easy option they might appear. If we do
decide to use them, we must:

- Choose with great care; always view before
  selecting
- Become thoroughly familiar with the film before
  using. Read any teaching aids supplied
- Choose the best point in the programme and the
  day; not just after lunch!
- Introduce with care, linking to other elements in the
  course
- Ask participants specific questions to be answered
  from what they see
- After showing, obtain answers and lead an active
  discussion on the film

There are a number of suppliers of training videos/films, all
of whom provide comprehensive catalogues and preview
facilities.

Games
Apart from the use of mechanical simulators we considered
yesterday, it is possible to simulate a range of situations
through the use of games. They can be used as an aid to
training in aspects of management and commercial decision-
making, and skills such as negotiation. The games will

usually be played competitively by two or more teams, and the results scored. They can be of any degree of complexity, from a series of choices dependent on the throw of a dice, through board games, many of which have similarities with the well-known 'Monopoly', to sophisticated and complex computer-based games.

Well-chosen games can be of help in appropriate kinds of training, and are probably an under-used technique. Several organisations are able to supply games.

Handouts
Whatever other techniques are used, the issue of handouts summarising the input of the event is almost always necessary. They minimise the need to take notes, and participants expect them. On the other hand, they are of little practical value in most training situations, and can, if handed out during a session, be a distraction. They are also rarely referred to afterwards.

The timetable

The sequence of sessions and the amount of time allocated to each must be planned with care. We should bear in mind the outline of the timetable throughout the planning process; it is a good idea to block in the time available at the start. A common pattern is four main sessions of an hour and a half each, split by coffee and tea breaks and lunch. The main sessions can, of course, be used as a whole for longer exercises, or split into shorter sessions.

It is crucial not to overestimate the span of attention that we can expect from trainees. This will vary according to many factors; the more interesting the material and the more participative the method of delivery, the longer it will be. For formal lectures, we should never reckon on more than 20 minutes, and much less after lunch or at the end of the day. For a well-planned group exercise, two hours is about the limit.

There is a greater danger of providing too much material than too little.

Guidelines for effective timetabling include:

- Follow a logical sequence as far as possible
- Theory should usually come before exercises,
- Never plan for more than 20 minutes of unbroken lecture
- Allow adequate time for introduction and briefing for exercises
- Hold extra material in reserve
- Use active exercises during the period after lunch
- Don't publish a detailed timetable

Summary

- In designing courses, we must always bear in mind the psychology of learning, and provide positive motivation, a familiar starting point, meaningful material, insight and reinforcement. In particular, we must remember the characteristics of adult trainees
- Planning content must begin with our objectives for the course and for each session. Old material can be dangerous
- We must consider a wide range of delivery methods, including: lectures, group discussion, case-studies, questionnaires, role-playing, demonstration and practice, in-tray exercises, videos/films, games and handouts
- The timetable needs careful planning

Course delivery

Successful delivery of a training course is as important as well-designed material. With bad delivery, first-rate material can be a disaster; with excellent delivery, even poor material can achieve much. We will consider training delivery under a number of headings:

Course delivery
- Setting up
- The start
- Classroom styles
- Lecturing
- Exercises and case-studies
- Giving feedback
- Discussion leading
- Timekeeping
- The conclusion

Setting up

The trainer will have a lot to do before the first trainee arrives. Trainees have a nasty habit of arriving early, so we must be in the training area even earlier. If it is possible to complete our preparations the night before, this will be ideal. If not, we may feel the need to be in the training area at least an hour before the event is due to start.

There are many things to check before the start:

Pre-course checklist

- Do we have our own notes and other teaching material?
- Is all the course material present and correct?
- Are all aids and equipment in place? OHP (plus spare bulb), video, flipcharts (plus sufficient paper and markers), etc. Do they all work?
- Is there sufficient, suitable and correctly arranged furniture?
- Are the catering arrangements in order? Do the staff involved know when coffee/tea/lunch is to be served, and where?
- Are temperature and noise level of the area suitable?
- Is the introductory material available and properly laid out? Name badges/name plates, folders, writing implements, notepaper, lists of participants etc.
- Are any necessary syndicate rooms available, open and equipped?

The start

At long last, our trainees start to assemble. They will form judgements about the whole event based on their feelings within the first few minutes, and we must ensure that those judgements are positive. The event must appear organised, welcoming and relevant to their needs from the word go.

The normal courtesies are essential. If we have finished setting up, we can welcome people as they arrive, introduce ourselves, offer a first cup of coffee or tea and chat.

The introduction must cover certain essentials:

Introductory items
- 'Welcome to the such and such workshop' (Participants have been known to arrive at the wrong one, if there is a choice)
- Very brief personal introduction of the leader (some people prefer someone else in authority to do this; many prefer to do it themselves)
- Housekeeping details; break and end times, message arrangements, loos, catering, etc.
- Documentation, handouts/notetaking etc.
- Course objectives (best displayed on a prepared flipchart, which is kept visible)
- Style/format/basic approach planned
- Round of brief personal introductions

Unless the trainer and group already know each other, personal introductions are important. Apart from their obvious value, they give participants a first chance to speak, and the trainer clues as to the needs of the group, the character of individuals, and any potential problems.

Rather than going formally round the group, some trainers introduce variety. If this can reinforce the aims of the training, better still. In an interviewing course, for example, participants can be given time to find out as much as possible about their neighbour, and introduce him or her rather than themselves. On a public-speaking course, participants can introduce themselves from the front of the group.

However they are conducted, it is best to suggest a structure to the introductions, and give participants a few moments to think about what they will say. A typical structure might be:

Participants' introduction
- Name, (organisation, job title)
- Brief description of their present job/role/where they come from
- Brief description of their cv/background/relevant personal history
- The most interesting thing about them
- Why they are here and what they want from the training

Introductions should be kept short; two minutes each should be ample.

Classroom styles

Experienced trainers develop their own range of classroom styles. Different circumstances demand different styles, and we must get the choice right. Possible styles include:

- Tell
- Tell and sell
- Tell and discuss
- Participate
- Facilitate

Tell

When using this style, the trainer says, in effect, 'This is what you must know, and this is what you will do.' It is the classic didactic approach, probably used in its purest form by preachers.

Few trainers consciously adopt the 'tell' style, but it is seductive. Telling seems to offer an insecure trainer security; if we 'tell', we can hope to avoid arguments with trainees who may disagree, or even know more than we do!

Sadly, telling rarely works as a training method. It fails on virtually all the criteria for effective learning that we considered yesterday, and is especially inappropriate with a group of adults.

However, telling does have its place. Telling is the natural way of explaining the objectives and methods at the start of a training event, or introducing an exercise. But even here we must reinforce telling by using a visual aid (listing the course objectives, for example, or the briefing for the exercise), and by welcoming questions.

Trainers sometimes slip into a telling style under pressure, either because they feel threatened or when short of time. But the group is sure to spot such a change of style, and may resist it.

Tell and sell

When using 'tell and sell', the trainer says, in effect; 'I am sure that this is true. Let me convince you why.'

'Tell and sell' is more suitable than plain telling for groups of adult learners, who are not prepared to take new knowledge or advice on trust. The swimming instructor, for example, will not only say to the learner trying to float 'Keep your stomach up and keep your ears in the water', but may add 'If you spread yourself wide, there's more water to hold you up'. The trainer will not only tell someone learning buying skills 'Get the other party to name a price first', but may add 'The seller may suggest a lower figure than you had in mind.'

However, 'tell and sell' offers little to motivate the learner, and little reinforcement. The trainer's explanations are unlikely to give insight to every member of a group, and may be based on incorrect assumptions about the group's existing knowledge, skills or beliefs.

The swimming instructor would do better to let the learner experiment with letting the stomach sag in the water. The trainer in negotiation would do better to ask questions such as, 'Is it better for you or the seller to name a price first?' 'Why?' or by using a role-playing exercise to explore the point.

Tell and discuss

When using the 'tell and discuss' style, the trainer says, in effect, 'This is what I believe is true. Let us talk it through and see how you feel about it.' It is a style often used by tutors.

'Tell and discuss' meets most of the criteria for effective learning. Learners will be motivated by the opportunity to express and argue their views. Doing so will help them achieve insight; expressing views publicly is an effective means of reinforcing them. The discussion will also show the trainer how much the trainees already know.

However, there are limitations to 'tell and discuss'. It gives pre-eminence to trainers and their views. It may waste time by using wrong assumptions or unhelpful explanations before an opportunity for discussion is given. It is more valuable in learning knowledge than in acquiring skills. Discussion may turn into argument.

Participation

To participate is to take part in an activity along with others; the word suggests an active involvement from the trainee. It also suggests that the trainer is involved too, rather than standing aloof from the group. It may even hint that trainer and trainees are learning together from a shared experience. Participative trainers say, in effect, 'Let us share this experience, and in doing so make it our own.' They will set the agenda, and establish the framework for learning, but will not appear as the fount of all knowledge. Instead, they will stimulate the group to use its own resources, making clear that all have something to contribute. There will be no formality; no set lectures or question times, and exercises may be extensively used.

The participative style meets the criteria for effective learning. However, it also has some dangers. Trainers are exposed, and need to be secure enough to be humble. Controlling the group needs discussion-leading skills; we will look at these later today. Timekeeping can be a headache.

Facilitation

Trainers are sometimes spoken of as 'facilitators'. By adopting this style, the trainer says, 'I am here at your disposal, with certain knowledge, skills and other resources. Use me as you think best to help you learn.'

Facilitation is only appropriate in certain situations. The more experienced the group, and the 'softer' the subject area, the more appropriate it will be. Thus facilitation would be appropriate for a group of senior managers developing their interpersonal skills, but a 'tell and sell' style will work better with a group of recent graduates learning about the health and safety obligations of a manager.

As we said earlier, there is no one right style. Experienced trainers will have a range of styles at their command, and vary them according to the needs of the situation.

Lecturing

Lectures should be informal, infrequent and short, but whatever style and other delivery methods are used, the trainer will need to offer some input on both process and content.

WELL, JUST TO RECAP ONCE AGAIN...

Guidelines for lecturing to smaller groups include:

- Grab attention at the start with humour, relevance, challenge
- Use a clear structure: 'tell them what you are going to tell them; tell them; tell them what you've told them'
- Use visual and other aids
- Encourage questions and discussion throughout
- Don't go on too long – 20 minutes is ample time
- End crisply and dovetail into the next activity
- Give handouts at the end only

Exercises and case-studies

Exercises and case-studies are not self-workers; to get the best from them requires skill and attention to detail. Here are some guidelines for getting the best from them:

- Explain the objectives to be achieved
- Brief using a flipchart or handout
- Deal carefully with all questions
- Use process observers and brief them fully
- Be available to deal with queries, but don't interfere
- Warn groups if time gets short
- After groups have presented their results, give a critique of the content. This may be supported by a model answer, a subject expert, or someone involved in the real-life situation
- Get feedback from the process observers, and allow groups to respond if they wish
- Ask the course to help summarise learning points
- End by returning to the objectives

It can be helpful to use participants as *observers*. In this way, several groups can be continuously observed at the same time. When the group has presented its findings, they will be asked to give feedback on the process used.

Process observers should be carefully briefed. Their task will be to watch their group at work, but without becoming involved. The need to avoid content must be stressed. They should keep careful notes of what they see.

Giving feedback

Feedback is a vital element in training of all kinds, as we saw yesterday. The sources of feedback include:

- Direct
- Self-criticism
- Other trainees
- The trainer

Direct feedback
The observable results of an action can be described as 'direct feedback'. Thus if a batsman at cricket attempts to play a certain stroke and misses the ball, he has received feedback on his attempt. If trainee bookkeepers are unable to complete a set of accounts, their methods have given their own feedback. If a manager's attempts at motivation fail, feedback will be inescapable.

Direct feedback is the most natural kind, and for this reason can be very powerful. However, it has drawbacks. Incidental factors (someone walking behind the bowler's arm; a missing cheque, interference by a more senior manager etc.) may have (or may be thought to have) contributed to the result. It rarely clarifies the real cause of failure or success; *Why* did I miss the ball? *How* did I fail to spot the absence of the cheque? *Why* did the senior manager choose to interfere? Trainees may remain unenlightened, or come to the wrong conclusion. They may also become discouraged.

Self-criticism

We are often our own harshest critic, and a criticism we make of ourself is usually, by definition, accepted. (Occasionally, it may be made in an attempt to stimulate praise.) If made publicly, commitment to improvement is usually implied.

To be effective, self-criticism must be based on accurate observation and correct assessment; both can be difficult. Trainees practising public speaking, for example, cannot see and hear themselves. Trainee negotiators may not realise that the result they obtained was less satisfactory than they could have achieved. Some personalities find dispassionate self-criticism difficult; they may tend towards self-justification and become defensive. Others may be over-critical, and become defeatist and neurotic.

For self-criticism to work, the trainer must create a climate in which it can be open and positive. This may be difficult if colleagues or superiors are present, or if there is a fear that training behaviour will be reported outside the training room. It is vital for the trainer to set up a 'no threat' atmosphere by saying, truthfully, that nothing done or said in the training environment will be reported outside. Most trainers refuse to give reports on trainees, unless they are required for assessment or qualification reasons.

The use of video or audio recording is often a powerful aid to self-criticism.

Feedback by other trainees
Other trainees can be used to give feedback; in informal group situations this will happen naturally. This kind of feedback may be accepted more readily than if given by the trainer, unless interpersonal tensions exist. Participants giving feedback will be stimulated to observe closely, and analyse what they see, knowing that they must justify their comments. Feedback by participants can be structured by providing a checklist. Such a checklist for use during observation of an interviewing exercise might be:

Observers' checklist

Room and furniture
Did the arrangement help or hinder, and in what ways?   ☐

Introductor phase
Were introductions well handled? Was the interviewee put at ease? How soon was rapport established?   ☐

Structure
Was the interview well structured? Did the structure
work well? ☐

Questioning
Were questions well phrased? Were closed or leading
questions used? Were answers probed when
necessary? ☐

Giving information
Was the interviewee given the chance to ask
questions? Were the answers satisfactory? ☐

Conclusion
Were the next steps explained? Were commitments
avoided? Was the conclusion courteous? ☐

Feedback by the trainer

Inexperienced trainers are sometimes reluctant to give
feedback. There are certainly dangers which must be
avoided. We may replace the participative atmosphere with
a teacher – pupil or even adult – child approach. We may
offend the trainee, or the whole group. We may become
involved in fruitless and time-consuming arguments. We
may reveal ignorance .

Despite this minefield, trainer feedback is essential in many
situations. Here are guidelines to help:

- Judge how welcome and useful feedback will be. Avoid if unwanted
- Do not overload; discuss only important aspects
- Invite self-criticism: 'How do you feel that went?'
- Probe the answers given: 'What do you feel was the problem at that point?' etc.
- Say what you saw and felt; avoid judgement except on demonstrable facts: 'I didn't feel comfortable with your approach. It seemed to me that you were not sure how to cope with Fred...'
- Face disagreement head-on, but courteously: 'Interesting you should say that. I felt that...'
- Reinforce success, but avoid creeping
- Finish on a positive, forward-looking note

Discussion leading

The trainer must be skilled in discussion leading; many adult training sessions will have the form of a discussion rather than a lecture.

Here are some guidelines for discussion leading:

- Define the subject; write it up and keep it visible
- Generate discussion by asking challenging questions
- Avoid expressing your own views until others have had their chance to do so

- Encourage the shy and restrain the verbose
- Prevent splinter groups from holding separate debates
- Summarise at intervals and record points of agreement on a flipchart
- Draw to a close when time, patience or the subject has been exhausted

Leadership of sessions can be delegated to trainees. This provides variety, gives the trainer a change, and can be a powerful learning experience for the trainee. It may also make the conclusions of a discussion more acceptable to the group, as they will not appear to have been imposed by the trainer. However, the choice of leaders need care. Unless they are reasonably skilled, control may be lost and regaining it can prove embarrassing and difficult.

By breaking the group into sub-groups ('syndicates'), more people will be able to have their say and more have the chance to lead. If this is done, the arrangements for reporting back to the plenary session must be clear, and sufficient time must be available.

Timekeeping

Good timekeeping can be difficult. If, as suggested earlier, we have not published a detailed timetable, the need for exact timing is lessened. This is not cheating; it gives the flexibility to spend more time when the group needs it, and less when it does not. Every group is different, and what goes through on the nod with one may be a source of conflict or difficulty with the next.

Here are some guidelines for effective timekeeping:

- Don't publish a detailed timetable
- Build in sufficient time for briefing, handling questions, physical movement and feedback
- Divide material into 'Must' and 'Useful'. If time is short, use only the 'Must', if there is spare time, add more of the 'Useful'.
- Keep a close but not obvious eye on the clock; make sure you can see one easily
- Avoid showing signs of impatience; they can be counter-productive
- If time pressure builds up, tell the group. If practicable, offer them a choice.
- Respect the group's needs; adequate breaks, train times etc.

The conclusion

The conclusion of a training event is almost as crucial as its start. It will be one of the key impressions that trainees will take away with them.

Trainers sometimes try to finish with a sweep-up session, at which participants are invited to ask outstanding questions. However, participants often switch off in advance of closing time, and those who do ask may make themselves unpopular. If we insist on lengthy answers, we certainly will. A detailed revision session will suffer the same problems.

Some trainers ask participants to produce an action plan designed to continue, apply and reinforce their learning. The plans will need discussion, either by the whole group or in pairs. An alternative is to ask participants to commit themselves to objectives for further development. These can be written down, collected by the trainer, and followed up after an appropriate time period.

If the event has gone well, we can conclude by asking participants to generate a list of learning points. However, if success is only partial, this can degenerate into destructive criticism.

We should conclude by revisiting the objectives for the event and demonstrating how each has (hopefully) been achieved.

A course appraisal may help to improve future events. We should not insist on participants' names on the form, and offer the option of returning them by post to a third party. On the other hand, participants taking forms away rarely do return them; it is better to collect as many as possible. We will look at such appraisals again tomorrow.

Summary

- Setting up a course in advance can have a great effect on success, as it requires planning and sufficient time
- The start is crucial and must be systematic
- Trainers should develop a range of classroom styles for differing circumstances. Those available include; 'tell', 'tell and sell', 'tell and discuss', participate and facilitate.
- The amount of lecturing should be strictly limited; when employed, it must be skilled
- Exercises and case-studies are valuable in most courses. They must, however, be appropriate and carefully used
- Feedback is essential. It can be direct, self-critical, provided by other trainees, or by the trainer. Methods need careful choice
- Group discussion is part of most adult training, and discussion-leading is an essential skill for trainers.
- Good timekeeping is important; trainers should develop techniques for achieving this
- The conclusion is the second most crucial part of a course, and needs careful planning.

Use of training, evaluation and sources of help

Use

Training has no value unless it is put to use. Neither, trainee, manager nor trainer can opt out of this stage in the sequence. If the training is on the job, continuing involvement will come naturally. If it is off the job, it may be neglected.

Re-entry problems
Much off-the-job training is ruined at the point when the trainees re-enter the real world. The papers in their in-trays are heaped towards the ceiling. Their colleagues feel they have borne more than their fair share of work. Neither colleagues nor bosses understand what the trainees have learnt, 'That's all very well in the classroom, but we don't have time for fancy ideas; the department's overloaded as it is.'

If needs were properly assessed and clear objectives set, re-entry problems will be minimised. They will be even less if a team is trained together; all will share the same learning, and can support each other in its application. But active involvement of the manager and continuing support from the trainer are always needed.

Follow-up
Worthwhile skills can rarely be perfected during formal training; they will need practice and development. Trainers can often give only limited help during this phase, but they can:

- Send out follow-up literature or exercises
- Contact trainees on a one-to-one basis
- Arrange follow-up courses or sessions
- Offer telephone help-lines
- Hold evaluation sessions with trainee and manager together

Support

During extended training, trainees need support. The manager may have to relieve the pressures of the trainees' routine work, boost their motivation, and help relate learning to real life. Financial support may be necessary.

Trainees' families may also help. Genuine interest and encouragement can do wonders for the success of the training.

WELL, MUM?! HAND OVER YOUR END OF COURSE REPORT!

Evaluation

We have now come to the final stage in the training
sequence – evaluation. Training is often an act of faith. We
hope it has done good. Perhaps it feels as if it was a success.
But the evidence is often subjective and weak. In particular,
accurate evaluation of the training of managers and
professionals presents serious problems.

We will consider evaluation at four levels:

- Training efficiency
- Short-term effectiveness
- Long-term effectiveness
- Cost-effectiveness

Training efficiency

This is the professional quality of the training, irrespective
of its results.

We need to evaluate this for several reasons. The efficiency
of the training will provide one clue (though only an
indirect one) to its effectiveness. Full evaluation will not be
possible for some time, possibly many months, but there
may be actions that cannot wait. We may have to decide
whether to use the training for others, perhaps even whether
to pay the trainer. We may need to reply to a trainee's
complaint.

Training efficiency is usually evaluated by some form of
course assessment. The assessment may be completed

immediately at the end of the course, or delayed for a day or two so that participants have time to think about it.

The kinds of question to be answered include:

Training efficiency
- Were the administrative arrangements efficient?
  - booking and payment arrangements
  - travel advice, maps, car parking etc.
  - pre-course literature/instructions
- Was the facility appropriate and efficient?
  - reception arrangements
  - comfort/heating/ventilation/noise levels
  - catering/accommodation
  - equipment and visual aids
- Was the training efficient and professional?
  - content (session by session)
  - presentation (session by session)
  - handouts/other teaching material

Comments are of greater value than ticked boxes, and the form should encourage these.

We should not be upset about isolated bad appraisals; no trainer should expect to please all of the people all of the time. If, however, a consistent pattern emerges, or low ratings are given by more than two or three people, a real problem is indicated. In evaluating training efficiency, we must never allow ourself to believe that we have evaluated its effectiveness.

Short-term effectiveness

Measuring training effectiveness will depend on how easily
the behaviour in question can be measured. If it can be
measured, this should be done both before and after
training.

In manual activities, measurement may be fairly
straightforward; there may be some accepted form of
objective test. We will know whether drivers have passed
their test. If we are training shorthand typists we can
measure the improvement in their performance. It should be
clear whether trainees can use the new computer system on
which they have been trained.

In non-manual activities, measurement is harder, but the
more precisely the objectives of training have been defined,
the more accurate evaluation can be. If, for example, we
said, 'To become an effective salesperson', evaluation will be
subjective. If we said, 'To meet sales targets next month',
evaluation will be easier and more meaningful.

Questions to be answered in evaluating training effectiveness include:

- Were objectives set, and if so, have they been met?
- Is there an examination or test to be passed?
- Are there measures of performance?
    - speed
    - accuracy
    - rejects/corrections/complaints
    - creativity
- Whose opinions can contribute to evaluation?
    - the trainee's
    - the customers'
    - the colleagues'
    - the boss's
    - the subordinates'

Longer-term effectiveness

There is a danger that trainees may slip back into their old ways. This is particularly likely if:

Forgetting new skills
- The skills are not used regularly
- There is no management understanding of or support for what has been learnt
- Colleagues do not use or value the skills
- The skills were only partly developed during training and the trainee lacks confidence

For these reasons, we should evaluate training a second time some time after its completion. How long afterwards must depend on circumstances, but is likely to be between three months and a year. If we are following up training, as we discussed earlier today, then long-term evaluation will form a natural part of this follow-up. If not, it will need carrying out as a separate activity. The questions to be answered will be the same as for the evaluation of short-term effectiveness.

Cost-effectiveness

The days have now gone, in most organisations, when it was possible to commit resources simply on the basis that we thought they may do some good. Training can be costly. We must know how much we are spending, and have evidence that we are getting value for the money.

Cost-effectiveness can only be properly evaluated if we have first found measures of effectiveness. Failing this, we can do no more than establish the costs of training, and set these against a subjective assessment of the value. A checklist of elements of costs of training was given on p. 34. Against these must be set the value. The money value of training may be established from examining such factors as:

- Has organisational capability been improved, enabling it to undertake new kinds of work?
- Is work done faster, with savings on time or numbers of staff?

- Is quality improved, resulting in less re-work, corrections, inspection etc.?
- Have the costs of attracting and recruiting new, ready-trained staff been avoided?
- Has customer service been improved, resulting in gaining, retaining or getting additional work from customers/clients?

Finally, we must consider the other payoffs. We may feel training is essential in self-defence against competitors who are committed to training. We may see its main benefits in the improved motivation and commitment of our workforce. As responsible employers, we may feel a responsibility to train those who work for us. We may believe that training is justified as our contribution to society and the economic well-being of the community. These reasons are hard to evaluate, but for many, the real value of training is to be found amongst them.

Outside help in training

Many organisations offer help in training. These include:

- Government
- Employers
- Professional bodies
- The education sector
- Private providers

The role of the government

Because development and training is accepted as essential to a healthy economy, governments have for many years been involved in measures designed to promote it. In the UK, the first industrial training legislation was passed in 1964, and it has been followed by numerous and continuing changes.

It is easy to take a cynical view of the large bureaucracy that this has produced, and express doubts about its value in producing a better trained workforce. Some see a number of the measures as cosmetic attempts to reduce the number of those classified as unemployed. But we must know about the current state of training legislation so that we are aware of what bodies to go to for advice, what qualifications are available, and what financial help (if any) might be available.

In the UK, three Government Departments are involved in aspects of training; the Department of Trade and Industry (DTI), the Department of Education and Science (DES) and the Department of Employment (DoE). Each has its own schemes and initiatives, covering three main areas: training young people, training the unemployed, and training within employment. These include:

> *Some key current UK government training involvements*
> - Training and Enterprise Councils and Local Enterprise Companies
> - The National Council for Vocational Qualifications
> - Investors in People
> - Training access points

Each of these is now discussed briefly.

Training and Enterprise Councils (TECs) and Local Enterprise Companies (LECs)
Eighty-four TECs cover England, Wales and Northern Ireland, and 43 LECs cover Scotland. Each has a Council including prominent members of the local business community and a staff of civil servants. Their task is to raise the quality and quantity of vocational training within their area. Within this overall objective they have a wide freedom of action, and each has worked in its own way. They may provide grants to employers providing specified kinds of training, and support initiatives such as Investors in People. The Careers Service, which gives careers advice to school students and other young people, is now controlled by TECs and LECs. Most TECs and LECs provide career counselling and other support services for the unemployed.

The National Council for Vocational Qualifications (NCVQ)
This has the aim of establishing standards of competence for every kind and level of occupation. The objective is to

encourage workers of all kinds to train, and to be able to demonstrate their competence to employers.

To help in this task, about 170 Lead Bodies have been set up. Most Lead Bodies cover individual sectors (e.g. the Transport and Distribution Lead Body), but some, such as the management lead body (known for historical reasons as MCI, or the Management Charter Initiative) and the Training and Development Lead Body (TDLB) cover the relevant workers in all sectors.

The qualifications offered are known as National Vocational Qualifications and Scottish Vocational Qualifications (S/NVQs). The lowest level is designated 1, and the highest so far defined is at level 5, which equates to senior managerial or professional posts. They are awarded on demonstrated competence rather than theoretical knowledge i.e. whether an individual can show that they can do the job. For this reason, APL (which we discussed on Monday) is extensively used to give credit for existing skills.

Reaction to S/NVQs is still mixed. Some employers have been convinced that they provide a major motivator to their staff to train, and thus offer all the benefits of a well-trained workforce. Others are less convinced, and may be discouraged by the resources required and the increased danger they see of poaching qualified people from them.

The Investors in People initiative (IIP)
This was set up to encourage employers to develop all their employees. It is administered by TECs and LECs. Employers who meet a number of criteria in developing and training their employees can qualify for status as an Investor in People. The criteria cover many aspects of good training

practice, including public commitment from the highest level, planning, effective and continuing action, and the evaluation of results.

Training access points (TAPs)
The system of TAPs is based on computer terminals located at points throughout the UK – often public libraries or Jobcentres. The terminals provide access to a national computer database holding information on training courses.

The role of employers

Employees can only develop effectively with the full help of their employer. The employer must encourage, guide, evaluate progress and provide the resources of expertise, time and money. This willingness must apply to the employee's immediate manager or supervisor; it is of little help if training support is a company policy, but our manager has no interest in our development, or says he can't spare us for training.

An increasing number of enlightened employers are adopting a philosophy of continuing development for all their employees. Those who do so believe that only in that way can they remain competitive and their employees remain fully motivated. Some call themselves 'learning organisations' to emphasise this commitment to continuing organisational and personal development.

Problems may exist in smaller organisations (what are officially know as SMEs – small and medium-sized enterprises). In these, the time available for training is often limited by lack of cover for absent employees, and competitive pressures may limit financial resources. The government initiative known as Business Growth Training (BGT) is designed to help in this area.

The role of professional bodies

Most professional bodies take the closest interest in the training of their members, in order to maintain the standards of the profession and limit the numbers of those permitted to practise. Many provide support in training, usually including courses, publications and sometimes advice and counselling.

Virtually all professions now accept the need for their members to undergo Continuing Professional Development (CPD). In the past, it was possible for an accountant, an architect or an engineer to qualify at the end of their formal education – often in their mid-twenties – and practise for the remainder of their career without further training. But this is no longer possible; anyone who tried would rapidly become out of date.

The role of the education sector

As the name implies, schools and colleges of all kinds have seen their role as providing education rather than vocational training. The main exception to this is the further education sector, which has always provided many vocational courses. At management level, many university and business school courses can be seen as vocational.

Many degree and diploma courses include industrial periods which are, in effect, training rather than education. The distinction between education and training is particularly fine in this area, and many college courses are a source of highly relevant vocational training, whether in the evening, by day or block release or on short courses.

Private providers

There is a wide range of private providers of training. Many specialise in specific areas, such as shorthand and typing, computer skills or driving. Others offer public training courses, typically in skills such as selling or public speaking. A large number operate by providing 'in-house' training designed to meet the needs of their client's organisation. The most effective of these often include an element of consultancy to help establish the training needs and to provide follow-up in the implementation of the new skills.

Summary

- To mean anything, training must be put to use. There are many pressures that militate against the use of newly acquired skills. If the training is on the job, use will be intertwined with the training itself. For success, off-the-job training must have suitable follow-up and support

- Training should be evaluated. Its efficiency can be assessed by a post-course questionnaire. Both short and long-term effectiveness will call for more thorough evaluation, based on the objectives set before training. Cost-effectiveness must also be considered

- Outside help is available from a number of sources. Recent government initiatives include TECs/LECs, the NCVQ, IIP and TAPs. Many good employers now aim to provide learning support for their employees. All professional bodies offer support, as does the education sector. This is supplemented by support in specialised areas by private providers